DOG TREAT BOOK

LEARN HOW TO MAKE TREATS FOR YOUR BEST FRIEND

By Beverly Hill

Introduction

I want to thank you and congratulate you for choosing the book, *"DOG TREAT RECIPE BOOK: LEARN HOW TO MAKE TREATS FOR YOUR BEST FRIEND"*.

You're about to discover how to make healthy, simple, natural, vegetarian and vegan dog treats.

We love to pamper our pooches, and giving dogs the occasional treat or doggy biscuit is a way to show our love in a way Fido understands. Dog treats are also useful training tools. A pocket full of dog treats can be used while training a dog to heel, sit, stay, or any other such command.

Using dog treat recipes gives you unlimited flexibility in the quality and variety of dog treats that you provide to your dogs. Chicken, beef, lamb and rice are some of the more popular flavors of commercially prepared dog treats and foods but when you use your own dog treat recipes your flavor combinations are limitless.

You can use peanut butter and honey to create sweet treats that do not include meat or you can substitute any meat you choose into your dog treat recipes.

Thanks again for choosing this book, I hope you enjoy it!

ABOUT THE AUTHOR

Beverly Hill is a sociologist. She is the CEO of C.E.F Associates and formerly served as head of department of sociology in Premier Natural Resources Inc.

A graduate of Nelson High School also graduated from the University of Toronto with a B.A in economics and finance and holds an M.S from Cambridge University in public relations and PhD in sociology.

She has written many articles on human equality, animal rights, environmental issues, personal development and peace keeping in different newspapers. She has also appeared in many magazines and is frequently interviewed for articles on family, race, socioeconomic status, and how to survive in your environment. She has also worked on the importance of health of relationship between parents and children. Her book 'The Middle Child' focuses on the importance of the attention given to the children and what to expect from them. This book helps parents understand their children.

In addition to these works she is also the author of 'Surviving Alone ' which is about her own childhood growing up; she writes about her family struggles living on a low income budget and growing her own food to survive.

C.E.F Associates formed in 1999 in Idaho, USA she worked both nationally and internationally. This is a consulting company which has clients all over the world. Ms. Hill the CEO of the company is the main reason of the huge client base because of her servings in foreign countries.

TABLE OF CONTENT

Chapter 1

DOG TREAT RECIPES

Chapter 2

SIMPLE DOG TREAT RECIPES

Chapter 3

ALL NATURAL DOG TREATS

Chapter 4

CHICKEN JERKY DOG TREATS

Chapter 5

HOW TO MAKE AWESOME TREATS FOR YOUR BEST FRIEND

Chapter 6

REALLY SIMPLE DOG TREATS

Preview Of 'MIDDLE AGE CAREER CHANGE: HOW TO TURN YOUR LIFE PASSION INTO A CAREER'

Chapter 1

MIDDLE AGE CAREER CHANGE

Chapter 1

DOG TREAT RECIPES

Dog lovers may want to give their pet dogs some treats to reward their god behavior. Take your pick from these various dog treat recipes.

Dog biscuit recipes include peanut butter, eggs, and flour and bone meal. Cheesy dog biscuits include cheddar cheese, chicken broth, whole wheat flour, cornmeal and oats, while bacon flavored dog treats make use of whole wheat flour, milk, eggs and bacon fat for flavor. There are also microwavable dog biscuits that use a variety of flours including cracked wheat, rye, and whole wheat.

Vegetarian treat recipes include vegetarian dog biscuits which use peanuts for the dog's protein source. Vegan dog biscuit recipes and doggie Christmas cookies also include peanut butter, honey, cornmeal, and flour.

Copper cookie cutters in fun shapes, such as big and small dog bones, cows, roosters, and squirrels will make fine dog treats that you can make into biscuit treats for your four-legged friend.

If you love baking for your dog, there are breads and cookie recipes that you can follow. These recipes include: peanut butter, bones, chicken and honey biscuits, big boy beef biscuits, and everyday biscuits. Other dog treats include parmesan herb treats, apple cinnamon drops, whole wheat cream cheese Danish, peanut butter and honey oat crunchies, and beef biscuits. It is important to invest in high quality baking sheets that have a non stick finish to come up with these treats.

Kindly note that dog treat recipes should be healthy for both young and old dogs. These include gourmet biscuit recipes that are delicious, economical, and healthy for the dog. Remember that not all food that is good for human consumption is good also for dogs. Some food can cause allergic reactions such as itchy skin, rashes, coat problems, and dull, thinning hair in dogs.

Before following recipes for dog treats, review first the ingredients to ensure that they are safe for consumption by your dog. Please note that seemingly harmless substance may prove fatal to your dog.

Chapter 2

SIMPLE DOG TREAT RECIPES

Let's face it, dog treats can get pretty expensive and many of us have dogs that deal with sensitivities or allergies to certain foods. All of the recipes you'll find in this book are simple grain-free and easily modified!

FROZEN PUPSICLE

Ingredients

1. ¼ cup peanut butter (unsalted/no sugar added)

2. ½ cup plain yogurt (I used 2% Greek)

3. 1 ripe banana

4. 1 teaspoon ground flax seed (optional)

5. Splash of unsweetened almond milk

Directions:

Combine all ingredients in a blender. Blend until smooth. Pour into ice cube trays or small bowls (I used Kong ice cube trays & the bonze mini silicon tray). Freeze until solid. Remove from freezer 5-10 minutes before serving to soften.

Chicken Wild Rice dog Treats

Your dog will love these DIY chicken wild rice dog treats that resemble mini muffins!

Mint buckwheat Dog biscuits

I call these after dinner mints! The parsley and mint in these treats is great for helping with bad doggy breath. Plus, the entire batch fits on one cookie sheet for quick prep and cleanup!

Small Batch Peanut Butter Banana Dog biscuits

Simple, small batch Peanut Butter Banana - Flax Seed Dog Biscuits! This recipe is a breeze to pull together and is a nutritious snack for your dog.

Puppy Power Smoothies

Made with four simple ingredients, these Puppy Power Smoothies are filled with vitamins, antioxidants and protein. Plus, parsley will help with any bad breath your dog may have!

Cinnamon Bun Bites

You love cinnamon rolls, so we're guessing your pup does, too! These dog friendly ones are made with whole wheat flour to make them extra healthy.

Best of Breed Dog biscuits

These dog biscuits are actually vegetarian, but your four-legged friend is sure to love them whether he's a meat eater or not. They also include parsley to help refresh your pooch's breath.

Homemade Doggie Treats

What's the secret to these irresistible treats? Melted bacon fat, Yep, your dog will go wild for these.

Homemade Peanut butter and Banana Dog Treats

Peanut butter banana is one of my favorite combinations, and we're betting all you pups cedar Dog will love it as well!

Apple-Cheddar Dog Biscuits

These are the perfect dog biscuits to have your guest feed your pooch when you're having a dinner party. It's just like they're participating in the wine and cheese course.

Homemade Dog Treats

These treats are especially healthy for your pup because they have both heart-healthy oatmeal and virgin coconut oil.

Peanut Butter Pumpkin Dog Treats

Take advantage of the fall flavors with these tasty dog treats. You can also use brown rice flour to make them gluten-free.

DIY Dog Treats

One secret to making homemade dog treats quickly is to combine your favorite flour or flour mixture with pureed baby food and bake. It doesn't get easier than that!

Homemade Flax Seed Dog Biscuits

Grind the flax seeds in this recipe to make sure your dog gets the most nutritional value out of them.

Paw-Print Dog Treats

The shape of these treats reminds us of Ritz crackers, but you won't need to worry about mistaking them for the pantry staple. The brewer's yeast gives them a distinct smell and will make your dog beg for more.

Blueberry-Apple Doughnuts for Dogs

These donuts get their sweetness from the applesauce used in place of oil, making it a healthier treat for your pooch.

Dog Treat Birthday Candles

If you're celebrating your pup's birthday, make these edible pretzel candles that they can enjoy once the party is over.

Sweet Potato Dog Chew-Vegetarian Alternative to Rawhide

You'll love making this sweet potato dog chew recipe for your dog because sweet potatoes are loaded with beneficial nutrients like Vitamin E, Vitamin B6, Potassium, and Iron.

Since it's one of the sweetest of all the vegetables, just like the name implies, you'll have no trouble getting your dog to try this dog treat recipe.

Chapter 3

ALL NATURAL DOG TREATS

Ingredients:

1 Large Sweet Potato, washed & dried

Optional Equipment:

Food dehydrator

Instructions:

1. Preheat oven to 250 degree F.

2. Line a baking sheet with parchment paper.

3. Cut off one side of the sweet potato lengthwise, as close to the edge as possible. Cutting the side of the potato first allows you to then turn the potato onto this flat surface that you have just created.

4. Having a stable area to rest the potato will make it easier to cut the potato into slices.

5. Don't discard that first piece; it comes out just as yummy as the rest!

6. Cut the rest of the potato into 1/3" slices, no smaller than ¼'.

7. Place them on the prepared baking sheet.

8. Bake for 3 hours, turning half way through.

9. Cool completely on a wire rack.

Storing: Although these treats are dried, you will want to keep them in the refrigerator for up to 3 weeks. You can freeze them for up to 4 months.

TIPS & TECHNIQUES

Choosing the right Sweet Potato: You should find a potato that is uniform in its shape. This aid in the drying process as the pieces will be similar in shape, and will cook through at the same time. Also, try to find one that has fewer blemishes or bruises. While you're picking one to make a sweet potato dog chew, go ahead and pick some for the family, too!

Yam or Sweet Potato: You can use sweet potatoes, like we did or yams. If you are in the USA, most likely you will find sweet potatoes in your local market. Either way, this root vegetable makes a tasty dot treat.

Knife Skills: If you are a pro with a knife, you may not need to cut off one side to stable your potato. If that's the case, then by all means skip that step. However, for those of us who are handier with a pastry bag, than a knife, having a stable surface makes all the difference.

Cutting Even Pieces: One way to ensure your pieces are as even as possible, is to first rest your knife where you would like to cut. Then press down gently across the entire length of the knife. Make a slight cut, then press firmly on your knife from one end to the other, and cut all the way through.

Degree of Chewiness: Baking for 3 hours result in a soft, but chewy dog treat. If your dog prefers more of a crunch, then bake for an additional 20-30 minutes. When you take the sweet potatoes out of the oven, they may at first appear to be too soft. Let them cool completely on a wire rack before you decide whether or not to bake them longer. This is because they will continue to dry or harden while cooling.

Finished Color of Treat: Sweet potatoes can vary in flesh color when raw. So, when baked they can be lighter or darker than the chews in the above photo. The texture is what you need to be most concerned with. Bake longer or shorter for the texture that you dog prefers.

Parchment Paper: Parchment paper helps to keep the sweet potatoes from sticking to the pan during the drying process. If you do not have parchment paper, you can use baking safe aluminum foil. Do not use wax paper as it is not safe for oven use.

Parental Supervision: This is not a dog treat recipe that we recommend for the kids. Please use caution while using a sharp knife, whether you are young or young at heart.

Whether your dog has a need to chew or not, she'll love this all natural sweet potato dog chew. In fact, it's such an easy dog treat recipe, I bet you'll be making several batches at a time for your dog and all of his all natural dog treat loving friends!

Chapter 4

CHICKEN JERKY DOG TREATS

If your dog loves the taste of chicken, he will do back flips for chicken jerky dog treats. When you make a dog jerky recipe you'll be the most popular person on your block (at least with your four legged neighbors).

Making jerky for your dog is not a difficult process. These chicken jerky treats are a perfect example of easy dog treat recipes.

This homemade dog treat is an excellent training dog treat. Most dogs will be happy to follow directions for this healthy treat. This is one of the few dog treat recipes that you can give to your pet cats, too.

Ingredients:

Chicken Breast Fillets

1. Preheat oven to 200 degree F.

2. Lightly spray a baking sheet with non-stick spray.

3. Rinse off chicken breast and remove any fat.

4. Slice the chicken with the grain. This will help make the jerky even chewier for your dog. The slices should be very thin, about 1/8" to ¼" thickness.

5. Place the strips on the baking sheet.

6. Bake for approximately 2 hours (see note below).

7. Remove from oven and cool on a wire rack until completely cool.

8. Cut strips into bite sized pieces.

Storing: These homemade dog treats may not last long enough to be stored because they are so good. But, just in case they do, store them in the refrigerator for 3 weeks. Freeze any remainder for up to 8 months. Be sure to read our tips on storing homemade dog treats for more information.

TIPS & TECHNIQUES

Checking: The baking times will vary due to difference in ovens, temperatures and meat size. Your jerky treats should be firm and dry, not at all soft or spongy. It is safer to go a little extra dry and firm than for the meat to be underdone.

Cutting: Once the treats are cool; it's easier to cut them with kitchen scissors or a pizza cutter, then a regular knife.

There is so much flexibility when making your own chicken jerky dog treats. One of the best options is that you do not need to be restricted to only using chicken. So let's preheat the oven and go for low and slow for these tasty jerky treats.

Chapter 5

HOW TO MAKE AWESOME TREATS FOR YOUR BEST FRIEND

There is no end to the reasons you should make easy dog treat recipes, but here are a few of my reasons:

Time: We all are limited to the amount of time we have in each day. But there is no longer a time excuse, at least not with these recipes. Even with a busy schedule you can make easy homemade dog treats.

Experience: Not all of us are born with a measuring cup in one hand and a cookbook in the other. Sometimes cooking and baking can be complicated. So, if you fall into that category, easy recipes are the way to go. You may find out you have a hidden talent.

EASY DOG TREAT RECIPES CAN SAVE YOU TIME

Preference: Do you have a picky pup that would rather wait until you've made an in-depth dog treat recipe to let you know she doesn't care for that ingredient? Easy dog treat recipes are a great way to test out new ingredients on your little connoisseur. If he turns his nose up, well, you're only out a few ingredients and a few minutes. But don't throw them away! Give them to a less picky friend or to your local animal shelter.

Equipment: At times you want an easy recipe because you don't have special baking equipment or you don't want to clean them after baking! These easy dog treat recipes do not require rolling or cutting with cookie cutters, since doing so can be more time consuming.

Chapter 6

REALLY SIMPLE DOG TREATS

There are some dog treat recipes that are so easy, there's not even a recipe. They are more of an idea or a simple task. A couple examples are:

Hot dogs: Bring hot dog to room temperature, cut into dog appropriate size pieces (if you have a small dog, small pieces or a big dog, big pieces). We recommend turkey or reduced fat kosher hot dogs for the ultimate in yummy treats. As a side note, hot dogs in general are higher in fat, so keep the serving size limited.

Vegetables: Whether they are fresh or frozen, most dogs will gladly accept a green bean, carrot or other tasty morsel. Review the list of foods poisonous to dogs to ensure you are not accidentally serving an unhealthy treat.

Ice Cubes: Plain water ice cubes are a welcome treat on a hot day. But make those same ice cubes with chicken or beef broth and you'll have a friend for life. No matter if the broth is store bought or homemade, opt for low sodium and onion free versions. Since these are frozen, you can make a tray of cubes and save them for future acts of good behavior.

Chicken: Plain cooked chicken breast (no chicken bones, please) is a luxurious treat that will not soon be forgotten by any furry friend. Next time you are making a chicken dish for yourself, set aside a small amount to cook with no seasoning or oil. Let it cool, cut into appropriate sizes and freeze any remainder.

Conclusion

Thank you again for choosing this book!

If your dog goes crazy for peanut butter you can find dog treat recipes that include peanut butter and then modify the recipe to include even more peanut butter thus amplifying the taste. You can find dog treat recipes from a number of sources including the Internet, books in pet stores and magazines.

You may even find homemade dog treat recipes available in specialty dog food and supply stores that focus on making products with all natural ingredients available to their consumers.

You can also modify dog treat recipes to suit your dog's nutritional needs. Using the example above, you could opt for low fat peanut butter instead of regular peanut butter, if your dog is overweight. This gives your dog the flavor of peanut butter that they love and also provides you with the opportunity to create a low fat version of a favorite treat. Homemade dog treat recipes are a good starting point but they can always be modified to suit your dog's tastes or nutritional needs.

Finally, if you enjoyed this book, would you be kind enough to leave a review for this book on Amazon? It'd be greatly appreciated!

Thank you and good luck!

Preview Of 'MIDDLE AGE CAREER CHANGE: HOW TO TURN YOUR LIFE PASSION INTO A CAREER'

Chapter 1

MIDDLE AGE CAREER CHANGE

In a economy limping along with a high percent unemployment rate, it's not unusual for even the gainfully employed to test free agency and see what else might be available. In a 2009 Salary.com survey, when global financial markets were still plummeting, more than 65 percent of workers said they were actively looking for new jobs.

It's one thing to change jobs, something most people will do more than 10 times between the ages of 18 and 42, but it's quite another to change careers. Making the leap from a field in which you've been trained and have experience to a wholly new one takes careful consideration planning and the right expectations.

This is true of anyone interested in making a change, but what about professionals who have been in the workforce for 20 or 30-plus years? Baby boomers, born between 1946 and 1064, make up 40 percent of the labor force, and shifting gears later in life to focus on new career objectives can be challenging, but also rewarding. Seasoned professionals often have a different perspective than their younger colleagues. Middle-aged workers usually place more value on nonmonetary benefits, such as less stress, flexible work schedules and personal fulfillment, so when they're able to change careers they can make the jump to areas that are more professionally fulfilling rather than having to worry about how much they earn.

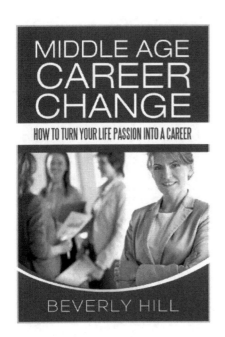

To check out the rest of MIDDLE AGE CAREER CHANGE: HOW TO TURN YOUR LIFE PASSION INTO A CAREER, GO TO AMAZON.COM

Check Out My Other Books

Below you'll find some of my other popular books that are popular on Amazon and Kindle as well. Alternatively, you can visit my author page on Amazon to see other work done by me.

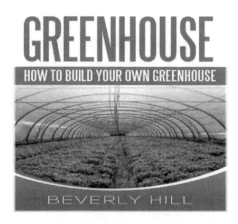

GREENHOUSE: HOW TO BUILD YOUR OWN GREENHOUSE.

GREENHOUSE GROWING FOR BEGINNERS: HOW TO GROW VEGTABLES AND FLOWERS.

You can simply search for these titles on the Amazon website to find them.

Bonus: FREE BOOK

Beginners Guide to Yoga & Meditation

So many people have achieved a sense of wellness they have never felt a since of wellness they have never felt before just through a few short yoga sessions. YOU CAN Download YOUR **FREE BOOK FROM THE BACK OF ANY OF MY E-BOOKS**:

NOTES

NOTES

NOTES

NOTES

NOTES

NOTES

NOTES

Made in the USA
Middletown, DE
16 December 2015